Life Conquering Advocate

Creator and Founder
Amy Pierce Romine is the creator and founder of Life Conquering Advocate. As a consultant and coach, Amy stepped into full-time mental illness and mental health advocacy in 2014. Using her experiences with a severe mental illness and her nearly 40-year walk with Jesus, she speaks out against mental illness stigma. As a mental illness and mental health advocate, she has become an award-winning blogger, speaker, Bible Study writer and teacher, as well as published author in about ten different publications.

Mission Statement
Life Conquering Advocacy's mission is to glorify God by sharing Amy's gifts (skills, experiences, and passions) to help tear down the walls of mental illness stigma with encouragement and education.

Vision Statement
Life Conquering Advocacy's vision statement is to provide life conquering encouragement tools to those individuals struggling with a mental illness along with those who walk beside them. In addition, educating a world that reacts out of fear to the unknown, thus perpetuating the cycle of mental illness stigma.

Mantra
Unbelievably blessed!

Core Values
Caring – for ourselves so we can care for others
Overcoming – barriers that make life hard to live
Noticing – triggers before they get out of hand
Quoting – words of affirmation, scripture, or mantras to re-center ourselves
Utilizing – the tools we have learned in order to dismantle triggers
Emerging – into the unknown as overcomers
Reassuring – it is okay to not be okay
Opposing – lies that perpetuate the cycle of mental illness stigma
Resting – our minds and bodies to have a clearer and calmer life
Seeking – to end mental illness stigma

1

Formal Education

Master's Degree in K-12 Principal Leadership and Science Education
Bachelor's Degree in Science, English, and Communications Education
Associate's Degree in Paralegal Studies.

Prologue to "The Calm in Your Storms"

I am super excited to introduce my second Life Conquering Advocate Bible Study. The study will focus on the account where Jesus falls asleep in the hull of a boat during a storm at sea. At the frantic begging of His shipmates, Jesus wakes up and simply tells the storm to stop.

Throughout this study we will discuss storms that arise out of nature like a thunderstorm or blizzard. We will also discuss personal, mental, and physical "storms". In the context of this Bible Study, the word "sleep" could be translated as reliance on Jesus.

The History of Our Bible Story

We find this amazing testimony to the greatness of our God in three out of the four gospels in the New Testament. There are two different Testaments in the Bible: the Old Testament and the New Testament. In the Old Testament, we are shown our need for a Savior. Conversely, the New Testament introduces us to our Savior. There are four gospels: Matthew, Mark, Luke, and John. The word gospel means "good news". The gospels tell the good news of Jesus, our Savior.

This account is documented in three of the four gospels. Someone might think the reason there are three different versions of this single account demonstrates the inconsistencies of the Bible. May I introduce a different way of looking at this appearance of an inconsistency through the following example?

Same Story – Different Perspectives

There is a car accident on the freeway. There were three different witnesses to the accident. In their reports to the police officer at the scene, do you think that each witness will give the exact same report verbatim to the police officer? Not exactly. It is difficult for each person to see the exact same accident, in the exact same way, at the exact same time, from the exact same perspective, process it, and retell word-for-word as each of the other witnesses.

In the same way, the disciples with Jesus would have responded differently to the storm surrounding them.

The focus of our study is found in

- Matthew Chapter 8 verses 23-27;
- Mark Chapter 4 verses 36-41; and
- Luke Chapter 8 verses 22-25.

Matthew was a tax collector. Mark was a companion to Peter later in life, so he wasn't even there when it happened. Luke was a doctor. Peter was one of the disciples on the boat when Jesus calmed the storm. If Peter wrote about it, his re-telling would have been entirely different, too. Why? Because he was a veteran fisherman. Each person had their own perspective to the same event.

The Purpose of this Study

We are using this story to study how we can manage the storms of our own lives.

During this Bible study we will address five key topics:

1. Why was Jesus able to sleep during the storm?
2. What are the components of a storm?
3. How does a storm in nature compare with a mental or physical storm in my life?
4. What do I need to do in order to sleep (stay calm) during my storms?
5. What does it look like to trust Jesus enough to sleep during the storms of life?

DISCLAIMER ALERT

Please take into account the following disclaimers in participating in this Life Conquering Advocate Bible Study:

1. I am not a Bible scholar nor do I have a seminary degree.
2. I have been a Christian for nearly 40 years. (I was baptized/gave my life to Jesus/accepted Jesus as my Lord and Savior when I was 9 years old.)
3. I have walked up hill and back, in the snow, barefoot with God by my side all the way.
4. By no means do I profess to be a perfect Christian. I have stumbled and skinned my knees too many times to count.
5. This Bible Study is written and delivered through the heart of a Christian who simply has a mental illness.

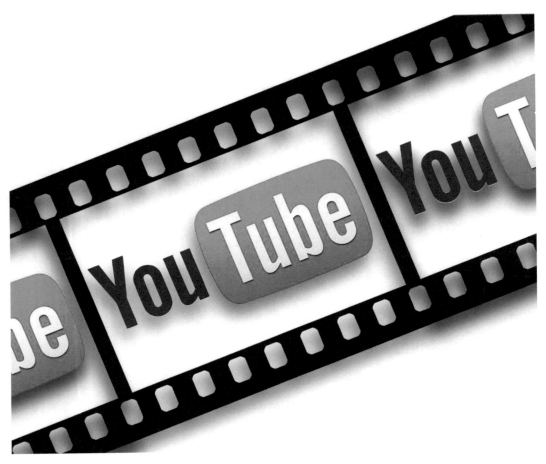

What to Expect from Me

1. I will stream live on my YouTube channel, @lifeconquering, the Bible Study discussions each week on Saturdays at 10 am ET.
2. If you are unable to make the live streams, they will be recorded and posted on my website, Facebook, LinkedIn, and Twitter.
3. Also, the date the Bible Study begins will be posted on the above social mediums.
4. During the live stream, I will discuss a few things including my own personal stories surrounding my journey with a severe mental illness as well as the role Jesus played in my "storms".

My Prayer for You

Dear Heavenly Father,

I pray for the individuals who will join me on this new journey exploring how they can rely on Jesus during the "storms" of their life. Please help them to know that whatever storms they may face in life, they are not alone. Help them to see You, God, like a lighthouse for a ship in the middle of the night during the worst storm at sea.

We are coming to You, Father God, with our hands and hearts open, seeking You to fill them with Your healing and loving touch.

In Jesus' name,

Amen.

Week 1 - Just the Facts

This week, we will familiarize ourselves with the biblical account of our study that is found in Matthew, Mark and Luke's gospels. I encourage you to use whatever translation of the Bible you are familiar with. Bible Gateway has over 100 different Bible translations. To make things easy, I will be consistently using the New International Version (NIV) for my scripture references.

Day 1

Read Matthew Chapter 8 verses 23-27.

Jesus Calms the Storm

23 Then he got into the boat and his disciples followed him. 24 Suddenly a furious storm came up on the lake, so that the waves swept over the boat. But Jesus was sleeping. 25 The disciples went and woke him, saying, "Lord, save us! We're going to drown!"

26 He replied, "You of little faith, why are you so afraid?" Then he got up and rebuked the winds and the waves, and it was completely calm.

27 The men were amazed and asked, "What kind of man is this? Even the winds and the waves obey him!"

1. If you were sitting on this boat, what would you experience in your five senses: sight, tastes, touch, sound, and smell?

    a. Sight: _____

    b. Taste: _____

    c. Touch: _____

    d. Sound: _____

    e. Smell: _____

2. Have you ever been awaken by a storm? Describe what it was like to have a storm wake you up from a sound sleep?

_____

_____

_____

_____

_____

_____

_____

_____

_____

3. Have you ever known someone who could sleep through a storm? If you ever knew someone who could, why do you think they were able to sleep through the loud claps of thunder that could shake a house?

_____

_____

_____

4. When you were a child, how did storms affect you? Were you scared or excited?

_____

_____

_____

5. Did you have someone that would comfort you? If so, what would they do to comfort you?

_____

_____

_____

Day 2

Read <u>Mark Chapter 4 verses 36-41</u>.

> **36** Leaving the crowd behind, they took him along, just as he was, in the boat. There were also other boats with him. **37** A furious squall came up, and the waves broke over the boat, so that it was nearly swamped. **38** Jesus was in the stern, sleeping on a cushion. The disciples woke him and said to him, "Teacher, don't you care if we drown?"
>
> **39** He got up, rebuked the wind and said to the waves, "Quiet! Be still!" Then the wind died down and it was completely calm.
>
> **40** He said to his disciples, "Why are you so afraid? Do you still have no faith?"
>
> **41** They were terrified and asked each other, "Who is this? Even the wind and the waves obey him!"

1. Note any differences you may have noticed between the readings in Matthew versus the readings in Mark.

   - _____
   - _____
   - _____

2. Think about the major differences between nature during a storm and just after a storm.

Nature During a Storm	Nature After a Storm

3. What is the worst part of a storm for you? Explain why.

_____

_____

_____

_____

_____

4. What do you think is the best part after the storm is over?

_____

_____

_____

_____

_____

_____

_____

_____

_____

_____

_____

_____

_____

5. What type of physical or mental "storm" are you encountering right now in your life?

_____

_____

_____

_____

_____

_____

_____

_____

_____

_____

_____

_____

_____

Day 3

Read Luke Chapter 8 verses 22-25.

Jesus Calms the Storm

22 One day Jesus said to his disciples, "Let us go over to the other side of the lake." So they got into a boat and set out. **23** As they sailed, he fell asleep. A squall came down on the lake, so that the boat was being swamped, and they were in great danger.

24 The disciples went and woke him, saying, "Master, Master, we're going to drown!"

He got up and rebuked the wind and the raging waters; the storm subsided, and all was calm. **25** "Where is your faith?" he asked his disciples.

In fear and amazement they asked one another, "Who is this? He commands even the winds and the water, and they obey him."

1. Note any differences and similarities you may have noticed between the three readings from these past three days.

Differences	Similarities

2. Describe the worst storm in nature you have ever experienced.

_____

_____

_____

_____

_____

_____

_____

_____

_____

_____

_____

_____

_____

3. Describe the worst "storm" you have experienced physically or mentally?

_____

_____

_____

_____

_____

_____

_____

_____

_____

_____

_____

_____

4. Why do you think Jesus pointed to the disciples' lack of faith?

_____

_____

_____

_____

_____

_____

_____

_____

_____

_____

_____

_____

_____

_____

_____

5. Do you think the disciples would agree or disagree with Jesus that it was their faith that they lacked during the storm? Why or why not?

Agree	Disagree
Why?	*Why?*

Day 4

1. Describe what it might have felt like to be one of Jesus' disciples during this storm.

_____

_____

_____

_____

_____

_____

_____

_____

_____

_____

_____

2. If you were on that boat and Jesus said you have little faith and basically there is no reason to be afraid, how would you react?

_____

_____

_____

_____

_____

_____

_____

_____

_____

_____

3. Portray your reaction when the storm disappeared when Jesus told it to stop.

_____

_____

_____

_____

_____

_____

_____

_____

_____

_____

_____

_____

4. Define your faith in God during a physical or mental "storm" you may have been through.

_____

_____

_____

_____

_____

_____

_____

_____

_____

_____

_____

_____

_____

_____

Day 5

1. Think of a recent "storm" or situation in your life that was difficult to overcome or manage.

    _____

    _____

    _____

2. Put a name to that "storm" (fired, divorce, anxiety, death, fear, COVID, OCD, abandonment, depression, migraines, fill-in-the-blank).

    My "storm" is _____.

3. If that situation were a natural disaster, what would it be (fire, flood, thunderstorm, torrential downpour, hurricane, etc.).

    If my storm was a natural disaster, it would be a _____.

4. Explain why you categorized your physical or mental "storm" as this natural disaster.
    I categorized my "storm" as this natural disaster because

    _____

    _____

    _____

5. Share your feelings and your five senses during this "storm".

Feelings	Senses
	Sight
	Touch
	Taste
	Hear
	Smell

6. If Jesus was with you during this "storm", what do you think He would do?

_____

_____

_____

Going Further

1. Look at your answer from Day 5 question number 6.
2. Why do you think you wrote what you did?
3. What is your answer based on?
4. Is your answer based on your own experiences, facts, or family traditions?

Why you wrote what you did for Day 5 question number 6?	What is your answer based on? Experiences, facts, family traditions, etc.?

Week 2 – How could Jesus Sleep?

Day 1

1. Take a moment to remember the events that occurred in Matthew, Mark and Luke's accounts of Jesus calming the storm. List three or more of them below.

   a. _____

   b. _____

   c. _____

   d. _____

   e. _____

2. Write down as much detail as you can remember from last week's readings.
3. Go ahead, you can look back if you need to.
4. Pick three (or more) key facts that stand out the most to you in these testimonies.

   a. _____

   b. _____

   c. _____

   d. _____

   e. _____

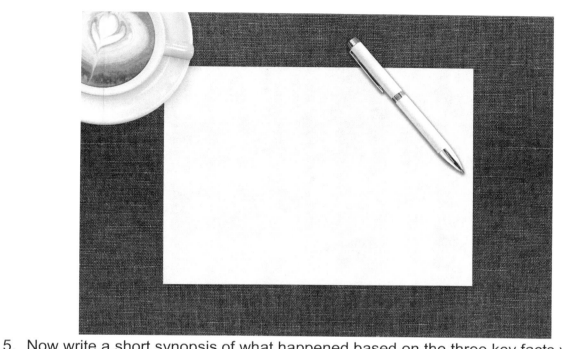

5. Now write a short synopsis of what happened based on the three key facts you picked out in question number four.

_____

_____

_____

_____

6. Describe the "storm" you are experiencing right now or have experienced in the past.

_____

_____

_____

_____

_____

_____

_____

Day 2

1. In Mark's account, he mentioned there was a crowd. In the previous chapter in Matthew's version, we see Jesus performing one miracle after another as well as moving from one crowd to the next.

2. How do you think Jesus felt once they decided to get into the boat? Do you think He was excited, frustrated, tired, or energized? Explain your reasoning.

_____

_____

3. Explain how you feel after you have been in a social setting for a long time? Are you energized or are you exhausted? Explain your answer.

_____

_____

4. What do you like to do to relax or unwind after a long day of stressful situations?

_____

_____

_____

_____

Days 3-5

Do you have flippers for feet or are your feet firmly planted on dry soil? When I was a little girl, we had a pool in our backyard. I loved to swim! I especially loved getting on top of a raft, floating and snoozing the summer afternoons away. Now, as an adult I am not that fond of water. If I had to get into a boat now, there would not be enough Dramamine to keep me calm.

During the next couple of days, we are going to look at some reasons why Jesus did not need Dramamine and was able to sleep during that horrible storm.

Before we begin, think of some reasons why you think Jesus might have fallen asleep during a storm on the sea that was so fierce His traveling companions thought they were going to die.

Over the next couple of days, I encourage you to look up and read the following passage from the Bible.

a. Genesis Chapter 1:1-27

The Beginning

1 In the beginning God created the heavens and the earth. **2** Now the earth was formless and empty, darkness was over the surface of the deep, and the Spirit of God was hovering over the waters.

³ And God said, "Let there be light," and there was light. ⁴ God saw that the light was good, and he separated the light from the darkness. ⁵ God called the light "day," and the darkness he called "night." And there was evening, and there was morning—the first day.

⁶ And God said, "Let there be a vault between the waters to separate water from water." ⁷ So God made the vault and separated the water under the vault from the water above it. And it was so. ⁸ God called the vault "sky." And there was evening, and there was morning—the second day.

⁹ And God said, "Let the water under the sky be gathered to one place, and let dry ground appear." And it was so. ¹⁰ God called the dry ground "land," and the gathered waters he called "seas." And God saw that it was good.

¹¹ Then God said, "Let the land produce vegetation: seed-bearing plants and trees on the land that bear fruit with seed in it, according to their various kinds." And it was so. ¹² The land produced vegetation: plants bearing seed according to their kinds and trees bearing fruit with seed in it according to their kinds. And God saw that it was good. ¹³ And there was evening, and there was morning—the third day.

¹⁴ And God said, "Let there be lights in the vault of the sky to separate the day from the night, and let them serve as signs to mark sacred times, and days and years, ¹⁵ and let them be lights in the vault of the sky to give light on the earth." And it was so. ¹⁶ God made two great lights—the greater light to govern the day and the lesser light to govern the night. He also made the stars. ¹⁷ God set them in the vault of the sky to give light on the earth, ¹⁸ to govern the day and the night, and to separate light from darkness. And God saw that it was good. ¹⁹ And there was evening, and there was morning—the fourth day.

20 And God said, "Let the water teem with living creatures, and let birds fly above the earth across the vault of the sky." **21** So God created the great creatures of the sea and every living thing with which the water teems and that moves about in it, according to their kinds, and every winged bird according to its kind. And God saw that it was good. **22** God blessed them and said, "Be fruitful and increase in number and fill the water in the seas, and let the birds increase on the earth." **23** And there was evening, and there was morning—the fifth day.

24 And God said, "Let the land produce living creatures according to their kinds: the livestock, the creatures that move along the ground, and the wild animals, each according to its kind." And it was so. **25** God made the wild animals according to their kinds, the livestock according to their kinds, and all the creatures that move along the ground according to their kinds. And God saw that it was good.

26 Then God said, "Let us make mankind in our image, in our likeness, so that they may rule over the fish in the sea and the birds in the sky, over the livestock and all the wild animals,[a] and over all the creatures that move along the ground."

27 So God created mankind in his own image,
    in the image of God he created them;
    male and female he created them.

1. Explain how this passage from the Bible might explain why Jesus could sleep through the storm.

   _____

   _____

   _____

2. Who created the sea? _____

3. Who created the wind? _____

4. Who created the weather? _____

5. If you created the sea, the wind, and the weather, would you be all that concerned if you were in a boat on the sea during a storm? Why or why not?

   _____

   _____

   _____

   _____

   _____

   _____

   _____

   _____

   _____

Week 3 – How could Jesus Sleep? *Continued*

This week, we will continue to examine through scripture why Jesus was able to sleep during a storm on the sea that was so fierce His traveling companions thought they were going to die.

Day 1

a. John 1:1-5

The Word Became Flesh

1 In the beginning was the Word, and the Word was with God, and the Word was God. **2** He was with God in the beginning. **3** Through him all things were made; without him nothing was made that has been made. **4** In him was life, and that life was the light of all mankind. **5** The light shines in the darkness, and the darkness has not overcome[a] it.

This can be confusing. The Bible teaches that God, the Father, Jesus, the Son, and the Holy Spirit are three in the same (1 Corinthians 8:6; 2 Corinthians 3:17; 2 Corinthians 13:14; Colossians 2:9; Isaiah 9:6; Isaiah 44:6; John 1:14; John 10:30; Luke 1:35; Matthew 1:23; Matthew 28:19).

1. Explain how the passage from the Bible verses above might explain why Jesus could sleep through the storm.

    _____

    _____

2. How does the verses from John Chapter 1 relate to Genesis Chapter 1.

    _____

    _____

3. According to John, who made the ocean and everything in it? _____

4. According to John, who made the wind and rain? _____

5. If you created the sea, the wind, and the weather, would you be all that concerned if you were in a boat on the sea during a storm? Why or why not?

    _____

    _____

    _____

    _____

Matthew 4:18-22

Jesus Calls His First Disciples

18 As Jesus was walking beside the Sea of Galilee, he saw two brothers, Simon called Peter and his brother Andrew. They were casting a net into the lake, for they were fishermen. **19** "Come, follow me," Jesus said, "and I will send you out to fish for people." **20** At once they left their nets and followed him.

21 Going on from there, he saw two other brothers, James son of Zebedee and his brother John. They were in a boat with their father Zebedee, preparing their nets. Jesus called them, **22** and immediately they left the boat and their father and followed him.

The Sea of Galilee was a bustling area of commerce and full of fishermen in the 1st Century. The life and career of a fisherman was very difficult. Someone who decided to become a fisherman needed strength and resilience to battle the unforgiving sea along with long days and nights.

Jesus had 12 disciples total. As we can see, the first four were all fishermen. Often in Jesus' parables, He used references to the sea and fishing since this was a well-known occupation throughout the areas He taught and performed miracles.

1. Explain how the passage from the Bible verses from Matthew Chapter 4 might explain why Jesus could sleep through the storm.

_____

_____

_____

2. Do you think these disciples were capable of managing a boat during a big storm?

_____

3. What do you think happened during this particular storm that we read about earlier in the week that caused these seasoned fishermen to be afraid for their very lives?

_____

_____

_____

_____

References
https://www.christianitytoday.com/history/issues/issue-59/fishers-of-fish.html

<u>Day 3</u>

Matthew 10:1-4

Jesus Sends Out the Twelve

10 Jesus called his twelve disciples to him and gave them authority to drive out impure spirits and to heal every disease and sickness.

2 These are the names of the twelve apostles: first, Simon (who is called Peter) and his brother Andrew; James son of Zebedee, and his brother John; **3** Philip and Bartholomew; Thomas and Matthew the tax collector; James son of Alphaeus, and Thaddaeus; **4** Simon the Zealot and Judas Iscariot, who betrayed him.

Here are a few facts about the Twelve Disciples:

- *Peter:* fisherman; although Peter denied Jesus three times he chose to be crucified upside down because he did not believe he was worthy to die like Jesus.
- *Andrew:* fisherman; passionate preacher; was crucified for his belief in Jesus
- *James (son of Zebedee):* fisherman; was one of Jesus' inner three friends; James was the first disciple to be martyred and the only disciple whose martyrdom was recorded in scripture (<u>Acts 12:1-3</u>)

- **John:** fisherman; was one of Jesus' inner three friends; wrote a large portion of the New Testament
- **Phillip:** was stoned and crucified for his belief in Jesus
- **Nathanael (also known as Bartholomew):** died as a martyr for his belief in Jesus
- **Matthew:** was a tax collector which was a profession most despised by the Jews; died for his belief in Jesus
- **Thomas:** a well-known skeptic among the disciples; died for his belief in Jesus
- **James (son of Alphaeus):** died for his belief in Jesus
- **Simon the Zealot:** a political activist; died for his belief in Jesus
- **Thaddeus:** died for his belief in Jesus
- **Judas Iscariot:** the disciple who betrayed Jesus for thirty pieces of silver (Matthew 26:15)

1. Explain how the passage from the Bible verses above, along with the information provided about these twelve men, might explain why Jesus could sleep through the storm.

_____

_____

_____

_____

_____

_____

_____

_____

_____

_____

_____

_____

_____

_____

_____

_____

Reference

If you would like to learn more about the Twelve Disciples of Jesus, the website below is a reputable reference.

https://www.crosswalk.com/faith/bible-study/who-were-the-12-disciples-and-what-should-we-know-about-them.html

<u>**Day 4**</u>

Mark 6:31

> ³¹ Then, because so many people were coming and going that they did not even have a chance to eat, he said to them, "Come with me by yourselves to a quiet place and get some rest."

1. "He said to them" is referring to Jesus speaking to His disciples.
2. Explain how the passage from the Bible verse above might explain why Jesus could sleep through the storm.

_____

_____

3. What do you do to rest after a stressful day?

_____

_____

_____

_____

4. If a friend came to you and said they had a very stressful day, what would you say to them and/or do for them?

_____

_____

_____

_____

_____

_____

5. What is your favorite thing to do when there is nothing to do – nothing to prepare for work, no housework, no errands, no shuttling kids to practice or games, etc.?

_____

_____

_____

_____

_____

<u>**Day 5**</u>

<u>Luke 5:15-16</u>

¹⁵ Yet the news about him spread all the more, so that crowds of people came to hear him and to be healed of their sicknesses. ¹⁶ But Jesus often withdrew to lonely places and prayed.

1. Verse 15 is talking about Jesus.
2. Explain how the passage from the Bible verses above might explain why Jesus could sleep through the storm.

_____

_____

_____

_____

_____

_____

3. Are you an introvert or an extrovert? Because of my bipolar, I am a little bit of both.

_____

_____

4. Describe the characteristics of yourself that make you more of an introvert or more an extrovert.

_____

_____

_____

_____

_____

_____

_____

_____

_____

_____

5. What do you think is the importance of "down time" for either an introvert or an extrovert?

_____

_____

_____

_____

_____

6. Do you allow yourself down time? Why or why not?

_____

_____

_____

_____

_____

_____

_____

Going Further

1. From the verses you read in the Bible over the past week and a half, what have you learned about Jesus?

_____

_____

_____

_____

_____

_____

_____

_____

_____

_____

_____

2. Jesus demonstrates His ability to stay so calm from within that He sleeps through a storm. You might not actually sleep through your physical or mental "storm", but sleep could be translated in the context of this Bible Study as reliance on Jesus. Do you think it is possible for you to rely on Jesus during your "storm"? Why or why not?

_____

_____

_____

_____

_____

_____

_____

_____

_____

_____

_____

3. How can you show reliance on Jesus through your "storms" or even your everyday life?

_____

_____

_____

_____

_____

_____

_____

_____

_____

_____

_____

_____

_____

_____

_____

<u>Week 4 – How could Jesus Sleep?</u> *continued*

You have had a chance to read some verses from the Bible regarding Jesus. Based on the readings and your journaling, spend some time in prayer each day this week as you try to learn from the Holy Spirit how you should "sleep" or rely on Jesus during your "storms".

<u>Day 1</u>

1. Write down why you think Jesus was able to sleep on the boat during the storm. Be sure you use the facts from what you read in the Bible verses from weeks 2 and 3.

_____

_____

_____

_____

_____

Day 2

1. I believe Jesus was able to sleep during the storm because of the following:
   - Jesus created the wind, waves, and the sea creatures. He created them, so He can also control them.
   - Some of Jesus' fellow companions were expert fishermen. These fishermen had been out to sea multiple times and had seen all kinds of storms. Therefore, these men would have been more than capable of surviving the storm and keeping everybody in the boat safe and alive.
   - Jesus knew the hearts of these men (Psalm 139). He knew these men would eventually give up their lives because of their belief in Jesus.
   - Jesus was simply exhausted. I am a heavy sleeper and can sleep through just about anything. If Jesus is God in human flesh (John 1:14 and John 10:30), He had zero fear in this situation. Due to His lack of fear, Jesus would have been able to sleep like a baby.
   - Lastly, if Jesus is the Son of God (Luke 1:35), He knows that He is ultimately in God's hands and does not need to worry about anything.

2. Compare your thoughts to the reasons I shared above.

Your Thoughts	My Thoughts
	Jesus created the wind, waves, and the sea creatures. He created it, so He can also control it.
	Some of Jesus' fellow companions were expert fishermen. These fishermen had been out to sea multiple times and have seen all kinds of storms; therefore, these men would have been more than capable of surviving the storm.
	Jesus knew the hearts of these men (Psalm 139). He knew these men would eventually give their lives because of their belief in Jesus.
	Jesus was simply exhausted. I am a heavy sleeper and can sleep through just about anything. If Jesus is God in human flesh (John 1:14 and John 10:30), He had zero fear in this situation. Due to His lack of fear, Jesus would have been able to sleep like a baby.
	Lastly, if Jesus is the Son of God (Luke 1:35), He knows that He is ultimately in God's hands and does not need to worry about anything.

3. Using your thoughts and reasons why Jesus was able to sleep during the storm, how can you "sleep" through your "storm"? Meaning, how can you rely on Jesus during the "storms" of your life?

_____

_____

_____

_____

_____

_____

_____

_____

_____

_____

_____

_____

_____

Day 3

1. Imagine what it would have been like to see Jesus sleeping during this storm that was so strong that these expert fishermen were afraid for their very lives.
2. What would you have done if you were riding on that same boat?

_____

_____

_____

_____

_____

_____

_____

_____

_____

_____

_____

3. Explain what it feels like in the middle of your "storm" (divorce, death in the family, job loss, unpaid bills) when you feel like "God is sleeping on the job"?

_____

_____

_____

_____

_____

_____

_____

_____

_____

_____

4. What would you say to God in the middle of your "storm" right now?

_____

_____

_____

_____

_____

_____

_____

_____

_____

_____

_____

_____

Day 4

Using your imagination, feel the boat being tossed back and forth, hear the wooden planks groan under your feet, see the masts sway back and forth. Can you also see the lightning flash across the sky, hear the thunder vibrate inside your eardrums, feel the rain pelt your face like tiny shards of glass, and the waves fight to pull you down to the depths of the sea?

Take a moment to soak it all in.

Write in the space what you are feeling and thinking right now.

_____

_____

_____

_____

_____

_____

_____

_____

Day 5

Put yourself inside that boat being tossed to and fro on the Sea of Galilee. In the midst of trying to stay afloat, you call out to Jesus to save you from drowning. Describe the scene the very moment Jesus wakes up from His much needed nap and simply calms the storm.

_____

_____

_____

_____

_____

_____

_____

_____

_____

Going Further

Take some time to journal your thoughts, questions, prayers, frustrations, or anything else you may have thought, felt, or experienced these past few weeks during our Bible Study.

_____

_____

_____

_____

_____

_____

_____

_____

_____

_____

_____

_____

Week 5 – Components of a Storm in Nature

This week, we will spend some nerdy science time thinking about what different storms are like in our world around us. You might not like science as much as I do, but hang with me! We will use the parallels between nature's storms and our physical and mental "storms" as we wrap up our study.

Day 1

1. List some different types of storms that happen in nature.

   _____

   _____

2. What happens during these storms?

   _____

   _____

   _____

   _____

   _____

   _____

3. Here are some interesting facts about weather:
   - Sandstorms can engulf whole cities.
   - Mudslides can carry huge buildings and cars.
   - Roughly 2,000 thunderstorms occur on the earth every minute.
   - Snowflakes in a blizzard could feel like pellets hitting your face.
   - Fire whirls are tornadoes created by wildfires.
   - A tornado can be faster than a formula one racing car.
   - A heavy snowfall or a "whiteout" can make it difficult to see.

4. What could happen as a result of the following:
   - Darkness

   - Rain

   - Thunder

   - Lightning

   - Wind

   - Blizzard

   - Hurricane

   - Tornado

   - Sandstorm

References

https://www.natgeokids.com/uk/discover/geography/physical-geography/30-freaky-facts-about-weather/

Day 2

1. Taking what you wrote about in Day 1, think of some impacts that a community or even a country may experience due to a natural storm.

    a. Economic

    b. Medical

    c. Infrastructure

    d. Nature

    e. Education

    f. Technology

    g. Food

    h. Shelter

    i. Other basic needs

2. How can your physical and mental "storms" in life impact the following:
   a. Economic

   b. Medical

   c. Infrastructure

   d. Nature

   e. Education

   f. Technology

   g. Food

   h. Shelter

   i. Other basic needs

Day 3

1. What wakes you up during a natural storm?

_____

_____

2. How do you feel when you are awakened during a storm at night?

_____

_____

_____

_____

_____

3. Explain the difference between a brief summer rain in the middle of the afternoon or sirens in Tornado Alley waking you up in the middle of the night.

_____

_____

_____

4. Imagine what our world would be like if we did not have the technology to predict changes in weather or various types of severe weather like tornadoes, hurricanes, or tsunamis.

_____

_____

_____

_____

_____

_____

_____

_____

_____

5. What wakes you up as a result of your physical or mental "storms"?

_____

_____

_____

_____

6. What things or people in your life could be considered a severe weather alert device during your "storms"? Why are these things or people a good severe weather alert for your "storms"?

_____

_____

_____

_____

_____

_____

_____

_____

_____

_____

Day 4

1. Determine why different areas around the world would have varying views about storms.

_____

_____

_____

2. Explain how and why location, intensity, and frequency have to do with severe weather around the world.

_____

_____

_____

3. What does a severe weather shelter look like for you and your family during a natural weather event?

_____

_____

4. What does a shelter look like for you during your physical or mental "storms" in life?

_____

_____

_____

5. Think about the physical or mental "storms" in your life. How would they be different if you were younger or older, married or single, have your dream job or just fired?

_____

_____

_____

_____

_____

_____

_____

_____

_____

_____

_____

_____

_____

Day 5

1. Think about a time when you were in a severe weather situation. Describe how old you were, what happened, where you were, who was with you, what you did to survive, how you felt, and what types of ramifications took place as a result of the severe weather situation. Explain the type of clean up that may have come as a result of this force of nature.

_____

_____

_____

_____

_____

_____

_____

_____

_____

_____

_____

2. Now, think about a recent or past physical or mental "storm" you have experienced in your life. How old were you, what happened, where were you, who was with you, what did you do to make it through the "storm", how did you feel, and what types of ramifications took place as a result of your "storm"? Explain the type of clean up that may have come as a result of your "storm".

_____

_____

_____

_____

_____

_____

_____

_____

_____

_____

<u>Week 6 – How to Sleep Through the Storms of Life</u>

This week, we will take everything we learned, put it all together and tie up any loose ends. We will not be learning any new material.

Our time will be spent journaling, writing prayers, or just praying silently or out loud. This week together should be a time to listen to what God is trying to speak to our hearts as a result to what we learned in the previous weeks as it relates to relying on Him during our "storms".

My prayer is for you to take everything we have worked through these past five weeks and see how we can "sleep" or rely on Jesus during our "storms".

Day 1

1. What is it about natural severe weather that is so scary or unsettling?

_____

_____

_____

_____

_____

2. What is it about our mental or physical "storms" that is so scary or unsettling?

_____

_____

_____

_____

_____

_____

3. How secure do you feel in your natural severe weather shelter? Explain your answer.

_____

_____

_____

4. How secure do you feel in your "shelter" during your physical and mental "storms"? Explain your answer.

_____

_____

_____

_____

_____

_____

_____

Day 2

1. Compare your "storm" in life to the storm the disciples experienced. For instance, did they feel out-of-control during the storm on the Sea of Galilee? Did you feel out-of-control during your "storm"?

_____

_____

_____

_____

_____

_____

_____

_____

_____

_____

_____

2. Switch places with one of the disciples. Have Peter or James take your place in your "storm" and you take his place in the storm we have been studying. Describe how each of you would react in the other's situation.

_____

_____

_____

_____

_____

_____

_____

_____

_____

_____

_____

_____

_____

Day 3

1. Has Jesus slept in your boat during your "storm"?
2. Explain your answer.
3. Why do you feel the way you do?
4. Write a prayer to God. Be completely honest with Him. It is okay to let it all out. It is not healthy to keep it all bottled up – especially when it involves matters of the spirit.

_____

_____

_____

_____

_____

_____

_____

_____

Day 4

1. If Jesus slept during your "storm", are you sensing that He is waking up to calm you and your "storm" now?
2. Explain your answer
3. Write a prayer to God or just journal. Be completely honest with Him about how you feel. It is okay to let it all out. It is not healthy to keep it all bottled up.

_____

_____

_____

_____

_____

_____

_____

_____

_____

Day 5

1. Use this time and space to journal or pray about what you learned about God, Jesus, yourself, and your "storms".
2. If you felt that God was not there during your previous "storms" or the "storm" you are experiencing now, how can you allow Him to be a part of your rescue?

_____

_____

_____

_____

_____

_____

_____

_____

_____

_____

<u>Meet Amy Pierce Romine</u>

Amy is a consultant, coach, published author, freelance writer, an award-winning blogger, Bible study teacher and writer, as well as speaker on mental illness. She is the creator and founder of Life Conquering Advocate where the purpose is to tear down the walls of mental illness and mental health stigma through encouragement and education.

She has articles published on the following blogs: Life Conquering Advocate, ADDitude Magazine, Psych Central, Blasting News!, and The Mighty. Amy is also published in a print magazine called *Today's Christian Living*. When she was a regular participant in her local chapter of Depression Bipolar Support Alliance (DBSA) she wrote monthly newsletters to share with her friends at the meetings. Her first Bible Study was on Anxiety which is available to be purchased as a paperback or on Kindle at **Amazon.com**.

One year into her marriage, Amy was first diagnosed as "bipolar" in 2007. After her diagnosing psychiatrist moved out of town, she bounced from psychiatrist to psychiatrist, off-and-on countless medications, along with therapist after therapist. Most of Amy's mental health providers did not believe she had a mental illness.

Amy's Advocacy is firmly rooted in the truth of what the Apostle Paul discusses in the Holy Bible in 2 Corinthians Chapter 1 verses 3 and 4:

"Praise be to the God and Father of our Lord Jesus Christ, the Father of compassion and the God of all comfort, who comforts us in all our troubles, so that we can comfort those in any trouble with the comfort we ourselves receive from God."

Amy does not have all the answers. She professes she is a child of God who has skinned her knees one too many times to count...who just so happens to have a chemically-imbalanced brain. At the same time, Amy stands on Jesus - THE Rock - who is immovable and unshakable even when her mind is spinning out-of-control with ultra-rapid cycling.

Made in the USA
Columbia, SC
14 August 2024

40467399R00046